NO WAY

NO WAY

An American *Tao Te Ching*

David Romtvedt

DAVID ROMTVEDT

LOUISIANA STATE UNIVERSITY PRESS

BATON ROUGE

Published by Louisiana State University Press
www.lsupress.org

LSU Press Paperback Original

DESIGNER: Mandy McDonald Scallan
TYPEFACE: Whitman

Thank you to the publications where these poems, some in different form,
first appeared: *Pilgrimage:* "The Master and the Waitress" (as "Gambling")
and "At the Creek"; *Psaltery & Lyre:* "Spiritual Mathematics"; *Rattle:* "Re-
membering the Wedding"; *The Singing Bowl* (singingbowl.org): "At the
Creek."

Cover image: Untitled, by Dollie Iberlin, 2020

Library of Congress Cataloging-in-Publication Data

Names: Romtvedt, David, author.
Title: No way : an American "Tao Te Cing" / David Romtvedt.
Description: Baton Rouge : Louisiana State University Press, 2021.
Identifiers: LCCN 2020027316 (print) | LCCN 2020027317 (ebook) | ISBN
    978-0-8071-7399-2 (paperback) | ISBN 978-0-8071-7512-5 (pdf) | ISBN
    978-0-8071-7513-2 (epub)
Subjects: LCGFT: Poetry.
Classification: LCC PS3568.O5655 N63 2021 (print) | LCC PS3568.O5655
    (ebook) | DDC 811/.54—dc23
LC record available at https://lccn.loc.gov/2020027316
LC ebook record available at https://lccn.loc.gov/2020027317

for Dollie Iberlin
with gratitude and love

CONTENTS

NO WAY

It was in high school when I first read the *Tao Te Ching (The Book of the Way)*, the sixth- or seventh-century-B.C.E. text by Lao-tzu that translator Stephen Mitchell has called "the classic manual on the art of living." The opening words have stayed with me:

> The way that can be spoken
> is not the constant way.
> The name that can be named
> is not the constant name.
> The unnamable is the eternally real.

Though that's not quite how Mitchell translated it.

Now I'm old enough to have been thought of in ancient China as a sage. That is, if I were in ancient China and also wise. For better or worse, I'm a twenty-first-century American and wise or not, in this country and time, a person of my age is simply old, notwithstanding the honorific title "Senior Citizen." I myself aspire more to trickster than sage though such an admission reveals an unseemly hubris.

All these years trying to approach what John Haines called "the owl in the mask of the dreamer," the God whose name I cannot say, the reality that stands behind reality, the words on the tip of my tongue.

I'm at the edge of the continent looking out to sea. I can't see the other shore or the person standing on that shore. I jump in and the waves roll over me, the undertow drags me along the bottom and spits me up once again into the air. I shake the sand from my hair and look back to see the next wave on its way. "Oh, Lord," I say to myself. "No way." But, really, I'm eager to be dragged into the ocean again.

Here's another way to look at it: I ride a bicycle. In winter, I float down a snowy hill, drifting as if I were sailing on a great white sea. In summer, I haul my daughter behind the bike in a lightweight nylon and aluminum trailer. But now my daughter is grown. I feel bereft, riding toward my dissolution. It's my attachment to my daughter, to the past, to the bicycle and my own legs churning that hurts. Still, it's not so bad to feel these attachments—I'm happy because of them. They are the source of the poems.

When I see a couple dancing—it may be the polka or salsa or zydeco or a simple Cajun two-step walking the way the old people do—one of the pair usually seems more attractive to me than the other. I once thought this was a matter of sexual orientation and fashion, but I now believe it is a more ordinary and universal longing for beauty. John Keats said that truth is beauty, and I thought he was wrong. I agreed with the poet Louis Simpson who noted the Holocaust and wrote, "There is the truth, you show me the beauty." Now I think both men were right. There is some entanglement of truth and beauty even if it is beauty that gets the upper hand. Or truth. My own father would beat me then go outside to tend his iris beds.

I see this in politics—I'm watching a political debate and I agree with one of the speakers, but I find the speaker I disagree with to be more interesting. I say to myself, "I'd like to talk with that person." I find the speaker's ideas odious while finding the speaker engaging. Once this contradiction troubled me. Now I find it thrilling as in this bit of a poem by William Butler Yeats: "O body swayed to music, oh brightening glance, / how can we know the dancer from the dance?"

I'm aware that this is a risky stance to take, that at some point I must embrace some ways of living and repudiate others. Lewis Hyde, in his book on the nature of the gift and the role of the artist, reminded us that in some cultures a person of substance is recognized for what is given, for being a vehicle through which gifts flow. In our culture, the big person is measured by getting rather than giving. If you start a dot-com company with four thousand dollars borrowed from your in-laws and sell the company three years later for a billion dollars, you are a success. But it's not just about money—you may also walk into a church or synagogue or school and kill several people by spraying bullets from the barrel of a semiautomatic weapon, fame and infamy having been conflated and both conjoined with success.

Ours is an age of exaggeration. Everything must be bigger, bolder, louder, longer, more nerve jangling and upsetting. Even the movies must be drenched in blood as the world itself, a thing as real as we are likely to know, is drenched in blood. Still, it is not helpful to be too cynical.

There is beauty everywhere and there remain people worthy of our admiration and respect. A tree is touched by its leaves and a dog by its fleas. The president is touched by her children and her children by the sting of life stretching out before them. The sky is touched by its clouds as the clouds find themselves touched by their sky. Perhaps there is one cloud and many skies. All beings are touched by genius. This is the same as saying there is no genius. Perhaps I've said too much.

DR

Buffalo, Wyoming

In the so-called Year of Our Lord 2021

NO WAY

The Names

No way I'm telling you
my secrets. I'm not even
telling you my name.
It's David.

The Lord told Adam to name everything
then said, "But when you talk to me,
there's no need to use my name.
I'm the only one here."

It's not as if things were so mysterious.
A fool knows that when he sees
the moon shimmer in the black water
of a midnight pond, it's not the real moon.

The sun rises and the water goes blue.
The moon, so clearly present moments before,
grows dim as the water grows bright,
darkness lending the other a sliver of light.

Unnamed

The wayfarer bends to drink—
muddy water, bad water, poison water,
no water flowing in the creek
with no name, over which,
birds, equally unnamed, fly.
Or are those clouds?

The trees along the banks
and the grasses. So many Adams
prowl the earth naming the unnamed,
maiming the unmaimed. Before God
lined us up in alphabetical order, Adam,
silent star in the vacuum of space.

Say Eve was first and Adam, carved
from the light behind her breasts,
rose to darkness, water dripping
from his body, Eve cupping
her hands, face wavering
in the stream.

The Master and the Waitress

I sat for a full day at the weekend zen retreat.
Ok, I got up for a drink of water and to go
to the bathroom. Then back on my cushion.
Made me want to scream. The master passed,
smiled, said, "Not great but not bad.
You wanta keep trying, right?"
I guess, but that smile.

Things were simpler in the old days—
the master whacked you with a stick.

A student picked the master up
at the airport. On the way home
they stopped for lunch. Wyoming—
nothing on the menu for the awakened.

"What'll you boys have?" the waitress
asked, wiping her hands on her apron.
The student ordered a small green salad—
hold the dressing. The master wanted
a double cheeseburger, onion rings,
and a Coke. When the waitress set
the food on the table, the master said,
"Excuse me," and switched the plates,
then added, "and a side of bleu cheese,
please." "Sure thing," the waitress said.
"Sorry about the mix-up."

The Well

Leaning over the wall by the well,
I look down into the dark water,
call my name, and wait for the echo.

I like to believe
I won't die until I'm ready.
It's a long shot.

Life is ephemeral,
even shorter,
driven by fear.

Remembering the Wedding

When a couple separates, it's hard not to stick
with one and let the other go. Sitting on the fence,
you risk being reviled by people on both sides.

A friend says, "My wife came home and found me
with another woman. I tried to make a joke, said,
'I got the laundry done.' Really, what could I say?"

"Nothing," I want to tell him, but keep still,
seeing the lover in bed, the washing machine,
the wife, the joke. Is that a joke?

His ex, also a friend, says, "I opened the door
and there he was with a woman I'd never seen,
each of them a bellows pumping oxygen on a fire."

I admire this metaphor made when she was angry
and hurt. And I've always thought her attractive
though it's not something I could tell her, even now.

I look out the window to the water, a tug
hauling a load of logs to the mill. The slices
of wedding cake laid out on their plates.

Rubble

I did my best, my mother told us, to protect you.
She means from our father.
Who could have known what would happen?

The planets revolve in space and when they collide,
the rubble scatters throughout the universe.

There's an image that will explain,
a picture in which everything is clear.

It would be easier if I could blame her.

Born

All this business about the eternal and the infinite.
They say what happened in the past is no guarantee
it has to happen in the future. They're talking
about war and maybe one day that will end.

As to death, no matter how much we've seen,
there's more to come. No escape. Well, Jesus,
but he's odd, the exception that proves the rule.
The only way out is not getting born.

Maybe I'm wrong, maybe we are infinite and
unborn floating forever in a vaporous nonplace
of nonbeing until we choose to come home.
With parents like mine, maybe stay in the vapor.

Do we wait as toothless babies or as the toothless old,
the first hesitant in the face of birth and the second
equally so in the face of death? Maybe it's midway,
that moment in which we become our imagined self—

healthy, happy, good looking, rich, no car crash,
no cancer, no war—see stanza one. Then the next
moment, the realization of delusion and, wham,
from drenched in infinity to drenched in afterbirth.

At the Creek

I go to the creek with my daughter.
We squat at the water's edge
and look around. Some pebbles,
a few sticks, a cottonwood leaf.
With these we make a tiny world
in which nothing moves.

Would that be heaven then
where all things come to rest?

It's as if I stand
once again by my desk
on the first day of school
and the teacher calls my name,
and I say, "Here."

She looks up and smiles
at me and I at her. "Here,"
I say again, "Here."

Sonetto Preoccupato

You can fill your bowl but if
you're eating sugar frosted flakes
and chocolate sauce it's diabetes you'll get.

Someone stabs you with a knife
or you step on a piece of broken glass.
Either way, your blood will flow.

Surgeons can replace most body parts
including a kidney or a damaged heart.
But the replacement—how long until
they find it and how to pay the bill?

Look, there's no point worrying yourself
to death. A million ways—I could tell
you—into the abyss. Worry to the core
and you can always worry some more.

One, Two, Three, Four

It's hard to focus sitting zen,
to stop and count your breaths
in and out from one to ten.

Most people can make it to four.

There's the phone ringing now.
I'll just answer it
and come right back.

You never know.
Someone could have died.

Or it's a warning—
a typhoon, typhoid fever,
type two diabetes, a tidal wave.

Really, the world's a mess,
growing messier by the minute.

I was explaining something,
wasn't I?

Comparative Religion

Say the universe is a car on a bumpy road
and the struts are bad—or springs or shocks.

It's time to head for the garage
and this far out in space, who knows.

There are some shops
where it'd be a mistake to take your car.

Hindu, Muslim, Buddhist, Jew—anyone
could be the mechanic—me. Or you.

We're in luck, that's God under the lift.
Looks like he's greasing an axle.

Wait, he's rifling through the manual
like he's never done this before.

What about the guy one workstation over,
porcupine quill shirt under greasy Carhartts,

gapping the plugs on an old Volvo, listening,
eyes closed? Hear that ping? Timing's off.

Vision

Drafted into the army,
I'm given a test for color blindness
and fail. "What then do I see?"
I ask the doctor.

"Hard to explain," he says,
handing me a sterile cloth.
"Lean back while I put
these drops in your eyes."

I've learned to name things
with the words normal people
use for what I've never seen.
But they're only words.

Red, yellow, green, and blue
swirling on the backs of my eyelids,
crows squawking in the silent sky.
I let out a little squawk of my own.

"What?" the doctor asks.
"Nothing. Only will this get me
out of the army?" "Get you
out of the army—that's funny."

He laughs. Now he can't stop
laughing, laughs so hard he starts
to cry, points at the sterile cloth,
blinks, mimes wiping my eyes.

Lion on a Cheese Grater

In many sex manuals, there are modest
pen and ink drawings of heterosexual
couples engaged in intercourse.

Positions are indicated and names
given to these positions. In the Greek
play *Lysistrata*, the women swore
to refrain from the position they called
The Lion on a Cheese Grater.

There's also The Ladder—the position
that entails the greatest risk of injury—
even when all four legs are stable.
People are willing to pay for pleasure
but how high a price? The books
are expensive. A sprained ankle
or a broken leg for the thrill
of sexual satisfaction?

When we stepped into our tiny boats
and set out to sea, the oars pulling
at the water, it wasn't so much sex
we thought about as rowing, the rising
awareness that it would be easier
than we thought to overturn the boat.

Drink

We're at this cocktail party
with a wad of local big shots,
the rich and powerful of our small town.

"Asshole," someone says
near the punch bowl.
We look around.

Paramahansa Yogananda tells us
no one can change an evil heart to good.
Just stay away.

My favorite Yogananda quote is about possession
of material riches without inner peace—
like dying of thirst while bathing in a lake.

It's true but here in Wyoming the lakes
are frozen half the year. The water grumbles
trapped beneath the midwinter ice.

In summer, the water's contaminated
by giardia—vomiting, nausea, diarrhea.
It's a risky drink, longing for inner peace.

Spiritual Mathematics

You can't trust a television
minister—it's the synthetic materials
in the suits, the church interior
a Hollywood reproduction of itself.

The great masters could be known
by appearance alone—bums on holiday—
their exteriors accurately mirroring
their interiors, whatever that means.

They were careful crossing frozen
streams or entering enemy territory,
not so much guests in the world
as birds flying above it.

The minister says that if I want
more money for my family, I should
give more money to the church.
This is called spiritual mathematics.

When you are hunting deer in the fall
and the snow begins to fly, at first
not sticking to the ground, later piling up
until your hat brim sags and wet snow

slides down your neck and shoulders,
will you sit patiently and await the deer?
Here the shy animal comes now.
See how it lifts its small dark feet

out of the shining snow, the tracks,
the cloud of breath. Maybe you
see it's not necessary to kill it
in the moment just after you shoot.

Empty Mind

Ignorance is bliss, they say. Smart people
are unhappy is how my father put it. Dumb
people are unhappy, too, I said. He shrugged.
The empty mind leads to the heart at peace.

Time to go home to what existed before
creation, before God spun himself into being
out of cotton candy, loneliness, and cactus spines,
Holy Trinity of the material world.

While all roads lead to Rome, it's a long trip
and if you run out of gas, you'll have to walk,
suffering blisters and thirst. But take heart,
on foot, you'll see more of what's along the way.

Weather

If you're a farmer, you put your fate
in nature's hands—rain and its absence.

Learning to read the sky
as if it were a letter from a former lover,
dull ache and longing, choices.

As to trust, there's federal crop insurance,
subsidies for certain fallow fields.

In drier climates, walking near sunset
along an irrigation ditch, moving canvas dams
under the long blades of light.

This is more treatise on government than poem.
I'm kidding. It's a poem. About weather.

Understanding Childhood

I tried to respect my father,
driven by fear.

Maybe it was good for me.
Toughen up, right?

I see a policeman
and turn the other way.

Eight o'clock Mass—God's
voice in translation.

Don't take me to a fundraiser
for a politician.

Passport, FBI databank, fingerprints, iris scan—
"Welcome home!" says the border control agent.

And school—the wind beating against the glass.
The waves growing louder along the shore.

Fewer Jews

The teacher calls the roll, asking us to say
"Here," and give our parents' names, what
they do to make a living, and what church
we attend. A half Anglo, half Chicano mob,
we're Catholics, two Lutherans, a Mormon,
and the weird kid who says he's charismatic.
The new girl, Miriam, says, "Here" like everyone
else then, "Jewish." The teacher says, "Class,
the Jews are the people who killed Christ."

Great grandmother was Sephardic. Afternoons,
when I got home from school, she'd pat the edge
of her bed. "Sit," she'd say, "and listen.
You know when Moses led the people out
of Egypt, parting the waters of the Red Sea,
we should have seen it coming—leaving Spain
for Portugal, east to Turkey, north to Holland.
I went farther—to Norway. I thought there'd be
fewer anti-Semites. What I found was fewer Jews."

Five, Six, Seven, Eight

Money and fame—I don't care.
Vintage cars, Cuban cigars—
there isn't any there there.
As for trips to Mars, I spent
my money at the county fair.

People get excited about sex
while I, without a boat, drift
along the shore where the carp
muddy the water as they mate.
I'm on my way somewhere.
No hurry, I'm already late.

The clouds stare down
at the ocean and the tide
rushes to the beach, nervous
waves shivering in the wind's
cold arms. Tumbled along
in the undertow, I come up
for air, sand in my hair.

What about dance lessons?
The fire may be out but
the ashes whirl in the wind
of former desire. I plunk
down my hard-earned cash
and am given a tourniquet,
told I'll have to cut off my legs
before the first class starts.

At the Dermatologist's

The dermatologist has perfect skin.
She wears a dress with a scoop collar,
modest but enticing, and given what
can be seen of her breasts, it's best
to focus on affordable health care.

My father was a master carpenter.
But he couldn't build a happy life,
hitting his thumb again and again,
blood darkening as it began to clot.

It's hard for me to keep my mind
on the precancerous cells spotting
my face, the dermatologist leaning
forward, inspecting my nose with
a magnifying glass, her cleavage.

The misery he carried through the day,
the jagged electric feeling around him,
the bomb in each hand ready to explode.
A man can love his pain too well.

There is something dark
and unfathomable about cancer,
even this not-yet-cancer-in-waiting.
"Treatable," she says. "All the same,
we want to be careful," moving closer.

My father is gone, swept into space,
but the angry molecules remain.
I look inside and there he is, jerking
like water droplets on a hot griddle.

It looks like the skin God would wear
if she were to come to earth, walking
in beauty while the rest of us, ravaged
by experience, turn and step away,
all too aware that soon we'll be dead.

At my wedding, he told stories, waving
his hands around as if they were songbirds
enraptured by flight. He was lighthearted
and warm, a man I'd never known.

Political Action

The president lies, calling it truth,
and the dictionary pages go blank.
The president sets race against race,
and the streets run with blood.
The president sees enemies everywhere,
and the corporations profit building prisons.
The president says, "My daughter is so hot,"
and the windows turn and look away.
The president announces victory,
and the gravediggers set to work.

The stones are sentient.
The water feels.
The sky remembers.

If you want to change
the system, you must turn
your back on it. Only then
will it disappear. It's not quite
that cut and dried, but it's a start.

Inner Life

Making the atom bomb,
we forgot
that nature, too,
might wish to guard it secrets.

We can say God's name
as often as we like.
Doesn't mean we know her face.
His. Its. Their. Oh, hell.

Falling leaves cover
the cobbles in the courtyard,
The earth
putting on its mask.

Every novelist knows
even fictional characters
hold something back
from their creators.

The squirrels gather nuts
for winter,
hiding a few
even from themselves.

Making an Effort

When my daughter first stood,
she wobbled.
And the first time she walked,
she fell.
Now she's dancing.

We all learn
though it's true that some
learn faster than others.

Some hurry, trying to catch up,
and find themselves falling farther behind.
Some can't pay for dance lessons.

I'm trying to explain
the workings of the universe
and this is the result.
On the other hand, if I don't try,
it's even worse.

Something Formless and Perfect

My mother's death floats before me,
the note she never wrote.

A trawler beats to shore,
diesel engine's excited roar.

Songbirds trace her path, salmon
thrashing upstream, the trees watching.

How confident we are—lying down
to sleep, convinced we'll wake.

Cottonwood fluff fills the hesitant air.
Blue sky expectant under red hills' stare.

No one is shouting.
The dew quivers on the grass.

As if the universe were serene,
nothing held back, nothing unseen.

The Conservation of Matter and Energy

Each morning I rise and set out for new lands,
mostly in my yard—I rarely leave home.

On my hands and knees in the garden,
I peel back the edges of the universe.

Thoreau joked that he had traveled widely
in Concord, his book resting in my hand.

Sometimes I walk around the neighborhood
at night, the streetlamps snapping on and off.

I look things up on the Internet—
pristine beaches, snow-capped peaks.

The teacher told us we can know a particle's
velocity or its location but not both at once.

Now my wife's kissing me in the back seat
of the car at the drive-in movie.

Another rainy night, vacuum wipers
sucking water off the windshield,

both of us still nineteen,
fooling around with physics.

Early Snow

The cottonwood trees along the street
haven't given up their leaves
but the temperature drops, and it snows
for the first time this fall.

I zip up my coat, pull down my hat,
and walk to the truck in the alley, get in
and crank the starter until the engine catches,
rough in the cold, pump the throttle, turn on
the defroster and wipers, wait.

While the truck warms up, I take a cigar
from my coat pocket and matches from the jockey box,
light the cigar, roll down the window, smoke.

I can smell the tobacco clinging
to the flakes of snow swirling into the cab.

The engine's smoothing out now,
the nasty vibration in the steering wheel
settling down. I put the truck in gear
and cruise around town, watching the snow
cover the sidewalks and streets, imagining
the other world into which I drive.

Oh, Boy

The American poet Frank O'Hara
said any old thing. You know—
I did this and I did that, rode the train
and it jumped the tracks and the tracks
are excited to be free like the earth
is excited to be in orbit around the sun,
the steel rail so hot I can't touch it
though I want to. Frank and I stroll
over to the movies, sit together,
hold hands. The lights go down,
the curtain comes up, the smell
of the fake movie theater butter
on our fingers, chocolate melting
on our tongues. Lana Turner,
James Dean, Billy Holiday—
alive forever, shining on the screen.
Dinner can wait. We'll picnic
by the water, the bright painted
boats tied up and bumping the tree
that rocks gently, the ducks bobbing,
hind ends in the air, faces in the mud,
chicken salad and a great big cake,
the sun slapping the clouds aside,
lemonade and ice cubes. We can
take off our socks. Someone wins
the big prize. Not me! I'll stop
at the train station magazine shop,
buy a cigar, step outside, look
at the marquee, and light up.

Making a Living

When I told my father, I would be a poet,
he grabbed me by the shoulders and shook me.
"Be practical!" he shouted. "How will you

make a living?" Shook me again. Harder.
My teeth rattling in my head, my father dead,
me getting older, poetry, making a living.

I was trying to improve things, believing
it would give me a purpose—my blood pressure
would drop, I'd live longer, be happier.

A beautiful summer day—I do laundry
and hang the clothes outside to dry,
the sun warming the shirts and pants.

For a minute, I worried the world
was perfect. If I tampered with it,
I'd ruin everything.

I'm still shaking, my teeth still rattling
in my head. Did I mention I was crying?
That I'm writing poetry?

The Day God Made Wasps

Fall and cool days,
digging in the garden.

The spot where I plunged
my hand into the still-soft soil
and came away covered by wasps—
arm, shoulder, neck, and face.

Now chilled, I sit outside
as one climbs my glass and leans
to the water, lingers to drink,
slender architect of the earth.

The masters allude to the keys
that will unlock the secrets
of the universe. It's a comfort
knowing there's more than one.

Second Thoughts

When the army called,
I refused to go. They said,
"Be a medic, help the wounded,
relieve suffering." I said,
"This too furthers war."

It was raining. A young man
lay on the ground before me,
hemorrhaging, his hands moving
as if searching for something
to grab, a door he could open.

My age. Maybe from a small town
like my own. Or a great unknown city.
Mist rose from the dripping leaves.
The blood spread, darkening his shirt,
shining on the surface of mud.

I thought I knew what to do.
Now I'm not so sure.

Ping-Pong

The problem with being a master
is expectation—the disappointment
when a master makes a mistake.
Even illness seems a personal failing.

In the West important churchmen
are often caught in sex scandals
or for stealing money but we
rarely think of them as masters.

"I am like you," the Dalai Lama said.
"Mentally, emotionally, and physically.
We are all the same." Maybe he enjoys
drinking coffee, watching the snow fall.

I forget for a moment the cruelties
of men, the gasoline I burned driving
to this talk. I want to ask the master
if he enjoys playing ping-pong.

He stands, adjusts his robes, removes
his tinted glasses, takes paddle in hand,
and gives me a look. The net shivers.
The ball says *pock* hitting the table.

Butterfly

Explaining that I had six months
to live, the doctor asked if I would
write about my illness. "Oh, no.
Too maudlin, I think." "Not at all,"
she said. "You're going to die.
You may as well speak freely."
Closing her eyes, she made a fist
and knocked me on the forehead
as if knocking on a door. What
would I write? I wondered.

That night, I dreamt of rain
soaking the fields, of mowing
the sodden lawn, and of failure.
Maybe I mean dying. Waking up,
the master said, "I do not know
if I was then a man dreaming
I was a butterfly, or if I am now
a butterfly dreaming I'm a man."
Either way, he woke up.

"It's your heart," the doctor said,
"full of holes." "Like a swiss
cheese," I said, making a joke.
"I guess." "Can you fix it?"
She shook her head. Butterflies
have hearts but no veins or arteries.
The organs float free in a sea
of blood. So I'm the butterfly
dreaming it's a man, the man
dreaming he's alive.

Carpentry

The universe being infinite,
there are infinite planets
more or less like this one.

On planet one, I'm building a table.
On planet two, a chair.
On planet three, a second chair
though there's no evidence
anyone else is here.

By the time I reach planet four
my wrist is aching
and my back is sore.

I'm not so much carpenter
as autodidact physicist,
gathering light from the stars
and nailing it to the walls.

Exam

Because the doctor recommended
self-knowledge over ignorance,
I sit on the bed, spread my legs,
and hold up a mirror.

Why are doctors mostly men?
Their advice is dangerous
whether you listen or not.

I guess self-knowledge
is better than ignorance.
Still, this eastern religion stuff—
masters, universal harmony,
the Great Way. They say
if you look for it, there's
nothing to see, if you listen,
nothing to hear.

Oh boy, here we go.
Hoping for a better view,
I turn the mirror to the side.
It's awfully dark in here.

One master is coy. Another mean.
A third is blowing smoke.
For the life of him, my doctor
can't say, "I don't know."
His mouth freezes up.

It's still too dark in here to see.
I'm gonna get a flashlight.

Withering Away

The Art of War, The Prince, the *Tao Te Ching.*
All these guidebooks to power and the state.
But, really, if you want to get rid of something,
you have to buy a trash can and pay the city rate
for garbage service. If you live in the county,
you'll need a pickup to haul your household trash
to the landfill where you'll pay a hefty dump fee.
Uncovered load? A ten dollar fine. Pay in cash.

To be free, beyond constraint—I don't know
if this will ever be but sometimes, late at night,
I look out across the broken earth, there below
the slow turning of the stars, their distant light,
and I hear the waves, smell the salty spray,
feel the ocean turning inside the dry hills.

Working

My neighbor never does a lick of work.
On warm days he sits outside drinking beer
from the can and reading magazines
he takes from waiting rooms.

When it's cold he wraps up—
wool scarf and hat, down vest and overcoat,
battery-powered socks and space-age gloves
thin enough to turn pages while preventing frostbite.

He tells me that if I sit very still
and am very patient I will feel the earth
turning. I say, "You don't have to make
fun of me." He says, "It might take all day."

From a lawn chair in the front yard, he waves
at the powerful men and women driving
to their offices downtown, preparing to change
the world, stirring up the leaves as they pass.

The Barking Dog

I walk down the alley and, as always,
the neighbor's dog starts to bark—
bark, bark, bark, I'm big, I'm strong.
But hey, let's get real—the dog's
eight inches tall and lives in a yard
surrounded by a chain-link fence.

Now and again the dog squats
and leaves a tiny mound of feces
in the grass.

My neighbor steps onto the lawn.
Looking at the feces while pointing
at me, he says to the dog, "What?
You've known him your whole life."

The dog goes on barking
while my neighbor, plastic bag
over one hand, scoops up the mess.

"Kind of a crummy chore," I say.
He says, "It's not so bad. I like being outside
when it cools off in the evening."

Taking the plastic bag from his hand,
he turns it inside out, twists the end
into a knot, and drops it in the trash can,
the dog still barking.

The Singing

The Tao speaks of clear skies
and things in harmony, life
without complaint or question.

The waves break
on the rocks. The birds
cry above the spray.

We, on the other hand, hold
our hymnals in our hands
and imagine a better place.

We brush aside the way
things are in favor of what
we call inevitable change.

We seed the sky for rain
and get a flood, blame nature
for being unpredictable.

That's the sermon, a warning
five thousand years old.
Let's move on to the singing.

Privacy

"Where do you get your ideas?"
a student asks when I finish
reading my poems to his class.

"My life is my own," I want to say
or something glib like, "Close-out sale
at the poem idea factory, online
from poemwriter.org, in the fog
during long walks on rainy days,
printed in extinct languages on clay
tablets frozen in glacial bogs."

Stuff like that.

But once even I was young
and privacy needn't be confused
with condescension. My ideas
come from God, an imaginary
being made from infinite affection.

The President, the Tao, the Day

When Donald Trump became president
of the United States, some people said,
"Oh, my God, you've got to be kidding."
Others said, "I don't know, I mean, yes,
he's a white supremacist misogynist
liar, I agree, but he says what he thinks
so I don't know, I like that." A few said,
"He will make America great again."

He said, "I moved on her like a bitch,
but I couldn't get there, and she was
married. Then all of a sudden, I see
her, she's now got the big phony tits
and everything . . . I'm automatically
attracted to beautiful women—I just
start kissing them. It's like a magnet.
Just kiss. I don't even wait. And when
you're a star they let you do it. You can
do anything . . . Grab 'em by the pussy.
You can do anything."

In the Tao, many passages are metaphoric.
The woman, for example, and the nation—
the leader who says he can do anything.

Twenty-five hundred years after Lao-tzu
wrote the *Tao Te Ching*—that miracle
of gemlike lucidity and deep wisdom
offering guidance in the conduct of life—
Donald Trump leads the free world.

The book lies open with its warning—
abandon the way and great beings fall
while the mediocre rise to prominence.
How prescient they were, those ancient
beings, how calm in the face of treachery.

The Train

I buy my ticket and walk to the platform.
I've got no luggage.
Who knows when I'll return?

I pass the first- and second-class cars,
the sleepers, and the dining lounge.

I was only pretending to go somewhere—
like window shopping, or dreaming,
or a child running away.

When I turn to go home, I see
the third-class car and get on board.

The windows don't open
and the snacks trolley doesn't come
down this far. There's no toilet.

The whistle blows and the cars jerk.
The station moves away through the smoke.

Action

Some days I don't do anything.
I mean, I'm breathing, and I have lunch
but mostly I sit around.

I don't have a theory about this,
like some people who talk about
nothing as something or emptiness
as fulfillment. I just sit around.

My father wanted me to be a lawyer.
My mother thought a Lutheran minister.
Sure, I said, sad to disappoint them.

I'm fine being told what to do
though I may not do it. Either way,
things happen—sky, wind, clouds
pushed away then pulled back.

It's like I'm explaining but honestly,
I'm just talking, listening to the sounds
more than to the words.

We Wanted to Know

I hadn't heard from Jimmy Durfin in years
when I got a package from his parents
telling me their son had died. So long
since those days in the ski-pole factory.
Jimmy's parents must be in their nineties.
We're old enough to be second guessing
the years ourselves—not Jimmy anymore
but the rest of us working the line, day
after day grousing and sweating, thinking
Goddam, this is my life? Man, I wish
someone had warned me. I'da left town.
Some of us did, got out to better jobs.
Others stayed, worked thirty, forty years.
How many remain? Us and the years.
It comes to that. Cleaning out his apartment—
Jimmy's parents wrote—he never married,
maybe you knew. No, I never heard from
Jimmy after I quit. We found these books
you'd written. We had a hard time tracking
you down. He must not be so well known,
we thought and apologize for that. We're
not so much readers but Jimmy read them.
He underlined passages and made notes
in the margins like in school before a test.
Actually, Jimmy wasn't much of a reader
either so we wondered if maybe you were
friends, if you knew him. That's why
we've sent the books. We wanted to know.

Dress for Success

I finally learned to tie my tie
so it's not bulging out on one side
and caved in on the other.

When I look in the mirror
it seems perfect but looking again,
it's not.

No time to fix it now—I have to drive downtown
for a job interview. I'm nervous—
the road twists and turns; it's easy to get lost.

Really, I should tie this again,
get it right, you know,
first impressions and all.

I could pull over and stop
but there's a lot of traffic
and I'm liable to get rear-ended.

The cars roar by and the light's
about to turn red. I roll down the window,
gun the engine, and shout, "Out of my way!"

Anything but Music

For years I sang only melody,
harmony eluded me. As for rhythm,
I had to use a metronome and even then
was convinced it sped up and slowed down.

My teachers suggested I study history
or go to heavy-equipment operators school
or join the army.

But I would not be swayed
thinking there is no greater defeat
than defeating oneself.

Now my thinking seems too easy,
having known defeats
greater than I could have imagined.

On the other hand, against the odds
and the advice of my teachers
I'm still singing, not that it's too late
for something else.

The Army

When I was a child, we'd sometimes
visit my father's army buddy.

The two men shook hands
and talked about the war,
forgetting I was there.
Or maybe not.

It was late when we drove home.
I'd lie across the back seat,
staring up as the trees ran ahead of me,
ahead of the car whistling through the night,
ahead of my father running before the past.

At home he was,
for a few days,
kinder to me.

Sitting

It's time for my daily meditation
but I live alone and have no one
to ring the bell so use a timer.
Bdrh-rh-rh-rh-rh, it rattles,
an operatic snake about to strike.

A rabid dog is chewing my fingers.
Sledgehammer blows crush my ankles.
My neck won't hold up my head.

I nod off and my face falls into my lap.
I jerk upright and look around
wondering if others smell desire,
forgetting there's no one here but me.

I don't have a master
so I get koans from a book
and solve them on my own.

The one about what was the face
you wore before this face. I collide
with the mirror and the glass shatters.
I could pull the shards out, but I think
it'd only make the blood flow faster.

It's tempting to look over
and see how many minutes
are left.

Keys

One day the master showed up
in a bikini. I didn't even know
he was a woman. The student
next to me said, "She's just
messing with your mind.
Keep breathing." I could
hear her counting in and out
up to ten then starting again.
Sometimes she'd lose count.
I do that, too. One to ten
while sitting quietly is not
as easy as it sounds.

When I lost my place breathing
I looked up and saw how pretty
the master was and I remembered
how kind he'd always been—kind
to the good students and the bad,
kind to me. He smiled and asked
if I'd drive to town and buy a case
of toilet paper. "We're all out,"
he said, "and enlightened or not,
we go to the bathroom." Then,
he reached behind himself to undo
the hook holding the bikini top
in place. "Ah, that's better."

"I don't have a car," I said,
looking away. "Take mine,"
she said, leaning forward
to reach under her cushion
and toss me a set of keys.
"Can you drive a manual
transmission?" "Sure, yes,"
I said, catching the keys.
It took my breath away,
the beauty of the open road.

The Moon in the Middle of the Day

Leaving her apartment for the last time,
the master turns, runs her hand along the door,
gives it an encouraging pat, hands me the key
and her winter boots. They almost fit.

The sun is blistering. An umbrella—
that's what I could use—or sunglasses
or a cowboy hat with a wide brim.
She drops her empty suitcase
at the Goodwill and walks away.

The friar who will be Saint Francis
is preaching to the birds, not the famous
sermon where they sit quietly in the tree
but the one where the nesting swallows
are shrieking so loudly no one can hear
and Francis cautions, "Dear sister swallows,
you've said enough, it's my turn to speak."
We settle down to listen and despite
the breeze, even the leaves are still.

Brother Francis repeats his message—
how lucky to have feathers though
we neither spin nor sew. How lucky
to have food though we neither sow
nor reap. And, oh, to fly. When Francis
stops, the master claps her hand.
The leaves remember to quiver
as the branches sigh and we stumble
aloft, hesitant fledglings pulled skyward
by the moon in the middle of the day,
gravity at a loss, the flap of our wings.

Playing with Words

My friend tells me not to trust
words, that words let us lie.
"We know the truth," she says,
"visible in every turn of the head,
lift of the hand, blink of the eye."

The anti-abortion activists say a fetus
is a full person with the same rights
as a person. Like a corporation.

"What if infinity is real?" I ask.
An infinite number of Adolf Hitlers
murdering an infinite number of Jews,
righteous souls, rare survivors, nervous
closets and anxious attics, secret wall
panels and false floorboards. Cruelty,
compassion, cowardice, courage.

"Disingenuous," my friend says.
"Cruelty, compassion, cowardice,
courage—you're like a schoolboy
who's just learned the word
alliteration and is showing off."

These words, I don't blame them,
where they come from and where
they go, the body a silent cocoon,
the ten thousand peaks rising beyond
the plains. This is not about abortion,
corporations, Hitler, the Holocaust.

"Do you never give up,"
she asks,
"playing with words?"

Reborn

It's nice to think we were somewhere
before we got here and that someone
brought us, a friend. Not that eternal life
offers an answer to our problems.

Up the mountain, unseen under boulders,
the creek sings its song of defiance, what
my mother called God's voice, only older.

I turn on the tap and the water, free
again, pours from the pipe. My mother
telling me not to waste, the bill to pay.

Then there's the sewage treatment plant—
swirling sludge and gray water, the aerators
and the smell of chlorine at the edge of town.

A brilliantly cold winter day, sun rippling
over the snow. Eyes closed, I lean into
the south wall of the house. The noise
in the sky fades, silence sings. Maybe
I'm exaggerating. Let's just say it hums.

Who could she have meant? My mother?
God's voice? How good we feel giving
things up—your house burns down.
You lose everything and don't mind.

The Road

The road is so wide you can stretch out
and sleep there though if you do,
you may be run over by a truck.

What kind of a fool would nap
in the middle of the road?
Even the deer run like hell
to get across.

In farm country, the road follows the fence line—
a long straight stretch then a ninety-degree turn.
At the corner, the cars slow to a crawl.
Still, the odds are good you'll be hit.

This is how the poor live
or refugees fleeing despots and war.
Even the middle class may find themselves
driven from their homes by fire or flood.

Life's a crap shoot.
Everyone knows that.

When spring comes you can see how hard
the winter's been—frost heave buckling
the asphalt, paint lines faded to invisibility,
potholes big enough to swallow a child.

At the Beginning of the Universe

I planted a juniper for your birth,
placenta resting near the roots.

We skated on the pond. "I can't stop,"
you said and fell laughing into the snowbank.

Together, we skied to your school
in early morning light and falling snow.

I read the Ramayana aloud—
you wanted to be the monkey king.

We climbed to the roof and saw
the winter stars through a telescope.

Then it was Christmas, the presents
wrapped in old newspapers.

This is already a good story
and it's only just started.

American History

Jimmy Durfin walked among the boxes
of bindings and poles, pretending to inspect
our work. Hardly a boss, he spent his days
in the back, smoking dope and telling stories
about Vietnam—the explosion in the tunnel,
the stick through the foot, the helicopter rotor,
how easy it is to long for what you fear, and
how the Buddhists fought on year after year
living on rice and wild onion. "It's believing,"
he explained. "They believed in something.
We, on the other hand, believed in nothing."
I could see my draft lottery number—61—
scrawled on the wall beside a cartoon face
and the words, "You're next, pal." Jimmy's
idea of a joke. Stepping down from an airplane
into the heat. Not that Jimmy was enlightened,
more like sleepwalking. But he knew things
I didn't. I think it was being stoned that made
him seem so calm, happy even. That's the deal—
for all his distance and cynicism, the stories
that made our skin crawl, he seemed happy,
oblivious to our dissatisfaction and the roar
of the machines—the punch press slamming
through a man's hand. He'd watch me crimp
a pole after the plug was inserted, pound on
the grip, line the dowel up in front of the drill
mounted upside down on the table and held
with a hose clamp, set the screw. He saw me
slip and drive the bit through the soft flesh
of my hand between thumb and forefinger.

Didn't report the injury. "Wrap it," he said,
and sent me down to packing. One day
Jimmy was gone, then me, never to return
to the bindings and poles, labels and baskets,
the crimper locking plugs to hold grips,
the drill, and the punch press coming down
through another man's hand, the quiet thud.

Making Ends Meet

You have a job, you can buy
groceries. Unemployed, you go
hungry. You can close your mouth
but it won't make the hunger go away.
Politicians tell you it's your own fault—
you're lazy, you have no gumption,
no get up and go.

Worn down by work, my mother
would fall into a chair and say,
"My get up and go just got up and went."
Joke all you want, there's still the groceries.

There were three of us kids
and my dad, I guess, makes four.
I don't know where he went.

Holding my hand, my mother
leans forward and looks around
without turning her head, slips
a package of pasta into her purse.

I can feel the pressure of her hand
over mine, the strength of her grip.

Framing

My father told me to stand up and be a man—
work my ass off and make something of myself.
Smart, fart, he'd say. Quit thinking a better job
will come along. You can't make life whatever
you want. Anyway, good and bad—who knows?
That's how he talked. So, it turns out my father
was a latter-day Zen master, out there in the heat
hiding nails, sweat running down his face.

Invitation

Pissed off, my neighbor waves
his daughter's wedding invitation
in my face. Turns out she's a lesbian,
making the bride and groom both women.

"Goddamit," he shouts, a little spit
flying across the fence. "Hey," I say,
you're not losing a daughter,
you're gaining a daughter."

"Fuck you," he says and turns away.
"I'm not joking," I say, "they're nice girls."

He's got a plan to break them up—
something about their jobs or a bank loan.

A few days later, he's back at the fence.
"You can't control the people you love,"
I tell him, and he says, "What're you,
some kind of television psych doctor?"
"I just mean you can't fix their morals
and trying won't make you any happier."

"Fuck you again," he says and heads
for the house. I say, "They're still nice girls,"
then reconsider. "I'm joking—they're rotten,
couple'a dirty lesbians." He lifts his hand
over his head, middle finger extended.

He'll be back—it's August, hot and dry,
he loves his daughter, and the wedding's
not till October when we start to harvest
the vegetables we planted in the spring.

Chickadees

I love the view from my kitchen window.
Doing the dishes, I watch the clouds, the rain
ready to fall, the chickadees in the spruce tree.

On warm days, I take off my shirt and sit
outside watching my chest rise and fall
as I breathe, the chickadees singing.

The old Chinese poets likened a woman's
breasts to peaches or plums. As for men's
vegetable metaphors, they had little to say.

There's the neighbor tanning on his side
of the fence. You can smell the sunscreen
he's slathered on, the smear of oil.

He takes off his shorts, looks at his groin,
grins, winks, says, "The masters say if you
feel guilty eating a doughnut, have a dozen."

I see him now and again at the bakery,
bag stuffed full. It's sweet, as long
as he stays on his side of the fence.

All this about the body, the neighbor,
the fence, desire, doughnuts, rain—
I haven't forgotten the chickadees.

Eating Fish

Like governing a great nation—
you have to get the bones out
or you might choke.

Pickerel and pike are especially bad
as is shad. And bones or not, you can
wreck fish by cooking it too long.

Some people complain, "But there are bones."
They buy canned sardines and eat them whole.
If you ignore the ticklish feeling, it's fine.

With a more delicious fish, you risk bloat
from eating too much, and however delicate
the flesh, the bones go in the garbage.

These metaphors—fish and government—
when I say them out loud, they sound good
but when I think about them, they fall apart.

A beggar enters a seaside village,
hands cupped before him. He doesn't ask,
"What kind of fish is this?" He eats.

Roses

There's my neighbor again.
He's not a power in town.
Most people don't know his name.

I'm not sure what he does
to make a living—something in an office.
He wears a tie.

As to his political views,
we talk about his roses,
how well they do in the heat.

We live where Arizona
and Sonora meet only now
they don't—the border.

There's a creek on the other side
and a hill on ours. We go there to sit,
watching the water we can't drink.

I want to tell him we should be free,
but I worry what he'll think,
and turn to the roses.

Center of the Universe

The Walmart's in the center of town.
It's unusual as mostly they build them
in vacant fields where corn once grew
and birds flew up behind clouds of bugs.
Now and again a blade of grass appears.

Rich and poor alike fill the aisles.
It's not so much treasure they seek
as bargains. Cheap stuff. Everyone
knows it won't last, life a lost receipt
blowing across an empty parking lot.

When a vast corporation is in decline,
people lose their jobs and when a new
corporation rises the workers are rehired
at lower rates. These changes are for our
convenience. Success is beyond all value.

People love Walmart. The aisles are wide
and well lit. No eye of a needle, no camel,
no rich man. The floors smooth and clean.
Can't find what you want? Ask. The doors
automatically open and all are welcome.

Not Me

I wanted to be an actor.
Not knowing who I was,
I wanted a big part.

My first play included a priest,
insurance agent, hanged man, waitress,
and a dying mother.

Later, I didn't care what part I got.
It was exciting just being in the show.
Once I was both murderer and victim.

I asked the director,
"If we're playing ourselves,
how do we prepare?"

Shutting Up

The great sages had one advantage over us—
they knew when to keep their mouths shut.

A leader who blurts out unexamined
feelings offends friends and enemies alike.

Silence says more than the user agreements
we sign before downloading new apps.

Lawyers question uncertain witnesses
and novelists invent unreliable narrators.

We don't need to say everything we think.
Sometimes we can rest, let someone else talk.

I'm just muddling along hoping
it'll come to me when to stop.

Hungry

After five years of school my father left.
He'd learned little of what they taught
but remembered his masters, young
women committed to the common good.

They had all the answers, if not
in their heads, then in the teacher's
guide that came with the textbook.

They didn't pretend to know everything
and were neither clever nor cruel. One
began at the beginning—the shape of an S,
the vowels A, E, I, O, U, and sometimes Y
as in sky my cry fly why, how zero
is the key to the infinite universe.

One rainy week the class stayed indoors.
Each child was assigned a state—
Oregon, Alabama, New Hampshire—
and asked to draw the state flower,
state bird, state tree. My father told me
he wanted to eat the wax crayons.

Hungry, it's hard to think clearly,
to untangle the knots of life, ancient
or modern. Imagine those Neanderthal
hunters singing their way home, dead
antelope over their shoulders, children
waiting in the classroom door.

Undertow

I'd like to be my own master
but that would make me my own slave.

Water never tries to flow uphill
although, evaporating, it rises.

In a world of competition, we begin
competing with ourselves. I both
defeat myself and am defeated.

It seems right to do the right thing
but the wrong may lead us farther along.

Better not to give advice,
especially good advice.

Teaching

I've been a teacher all my life
believing knowledge can change the world.
Not that it isn't changing all the time
but, you know, for the better. Be patient,
I tell myself still believing in knowledge
though I've given up a little on the better.

Fridays after school we went for beers
at The Little Brown Jug. Slightly drunk,
the history teacher said if we really taught
students critical thinking, we'd be teaching
social revolution. I laughed then frowned.

Administrators, parents, legislators,
even some teachers said we should
emphasize life skills—how to get a job
you'll hate and then how to keep it.

I taught poetry writing. "The world
is so fast and poetry so slow," I told
the students. "Let's sit for a minute.
Close your eyes. Notice your breathing.
Then write." A parent filed a complaint—
I was forcing religion on children—
and a reprimand was added to my file
but they didn't fire me, so I kept teaching.

Insurance Premium

My neighbor needed a kidney transplant
so I donated one of mine, further blurring
the boundary between self and other.

In the morning, when he steps outside
and heads for his car, he smiles and waves
and I smile and wave back.

At neighborhood barbecues, he offers
me a no-alcohol beer. "We're in the same
boat now," he says, and we drink.

At home I have a real beer.
I'm okay but one kidney down,
I'm a little anxious.

When my insurance company
found out what I'd done, they raised
my premium—greater risk.

It's hard to admit I'm annoyed
that my neighbor may outlive me,
that my rates have gone up.

Pawns

A wise general may think it better
to wait and see but if you're playing chess
someone has to make the first move.

The pawns tumble over the cliff
into the abyss without even
a pocketknife or a length of rope.
One makes it across the board
and like a poor man waking a genie
is offered whatever he wants.
He takes the queen, is the queen.

But it's a lottery—the chance
of winning slim to none—
the king protected by yes-men
and, nowadays, yes-women,
the bloody stink of power.

There's always someone worse off
than us, my mother told me.
Thanksgiving dinner—what are you
thankful for? I'm not arguing
for appreciating what you've got.

I admit I'm happy and expect to be
happier still. Only a fool clings to sorrow.
I have enemies and no matter what I do
some will remain so.

I try to leap over this fence,
put all my strength into it and jump,
throwing my arms high into the air,
my body not far behind. Maybe
I clear the top, maybe not.

Urine

I don't understand anything.
I say these words, but I don't
know where they come from.
I'm practicing but for what?

My teachers are so old
they can barely speak.
Some days they nod off,
heads rolling forward until
their chins hit their chests,
drooling onto their shirts.

It's as if they're looking down
at the dark stains spreading
on their pants, their bladders
letting go and the familiar smell
of urine filling the room.

No Lie

The Master of all things steps
into the sea of suffering and swims
in the dark water of universal healing.

She removes her shoes
and stands in the rain,
sinking into the soft earth.

The moon rises over the hills
that lean toward the sea,
drawn by the tide.

In the mudflats, a heron
stands as still as time,
waiting for a fish.

These little observations
sound great but as to what they mean,
your guess is as good as mine.

And all that stuff about knowing
and not-knowing as the shining gate
to true knowledge—who can say?

I don't know why
I should be lying
so late in the game.

Manifesto

Marx said that religion is the opiate
of the masses. How sweet, we think—
life after death, though science fiction
suggests eternal life may bring eternal
ennui, leaving religious longing both
touching and troubling. Marx, a man
like others, suffering hunger, illness,
sorrow, and death while the flocks
of the faithful continue to increase.

The young Karl's at the high school
dance in the gym after the game.
The band plays a waltz, the step
that has taken Europe by storm.
Karl's girlfriend whispers in his ear.
The logic is of love, but she says,
"You think you're better than me
because I believe in God." "No,
no," Karl says, worried not so much
about God as the bulge in his pants,
that she'll notice how hard it is
for him to express his feelings.

Let's forget Marx and God,
and waltz, the eternal self
caressing life.

The Net

It's not so easy being at ease.
Just about anyone can rattle off a list
of problems that'd give God an anxiety attack.

But we give it a try
and some do remarkably well,
answering the phone with a cheerful hello.

Confiding in a friend, saying,
"It's a secret. You understand." Spreading
pain as if it were butter melting on a piece of toast.

There are questions not worth asking,
trains that neither depart nor arrive, roaring
around snowy mountain curves through dark tunnels.

When a fisherman
throws a net into the sea,
there's no telling what may come to the surface.

The Nail

There's the story about the nail
that fell from the horse's shoe
and the horse threw the shoe
and the knight couldn't ride
and the battle was lost
and the kingdom, too.
For want of a nail.

Or the one about the butterfly
in Brazil that flaps its nearly
weightless wings and sets
in motion a chain of events
that ends six weeks later
with a tornado in Texas.

A fisherman hauls up a rusty can
or a shoe with no sole, a talking clam
that's really an enchanted genie—
"Fame, money, sex—what d'ya want?"
"A new net," the fisherman says.

Some people want more—
imagined plenty leading to not enough.
History rolls on. The books groan
under the weight of dead kings,
the nameless echo of those crushed
by the wheels of their carriages.

Extinct

For centuries, wise women and men
have advised kings and queens—
greed fueled by lies will become
kindling for ever larger fires.
Serve the common good, help
the poor and infirm, respect both
youth and age, love the earth
as you love yourselves, etcetera.

These comments on history and advice
on social structure—you have to think
about them. It takes a lot of time
and it's unclear if things are better
now than when the great mastodons
roamed the earth.

The Ski Poles

Sometimes Jimmy would have us do something
useless—stack cardboard boxes along the wall
then move them across the room to the other wall
or cut them open then tape them back together.
Busy work for the bosses, the poles to upscale shops
in Aspen, Colorado, and Jackson, Wyoming. I'd look
down at the piles stacked basket to grip and see bodies
in open graves, feet beside heads, snow, the leafless
branches of the trees contorted by wind, some dark
Polish village surrounded by fields of frozen mud.
At home, what little Jewish we were was Sephardic.
Everyone got out long ago—Spain, Holland, Norway,
the United States, my great aunt, face powdered white,
stink of perfume, my great-grandmother teaching us
Ladino which we never could speak. Jimmy would
grab a set of poles and make us pull the grips, check
the crimps holding the plugs. "It's like the fillings
in your teeth," he'd say. "Don't want 'em to fall out.
Every tip should be tight, ferrules smooth and clean,
baskets straight." I'd be standing there wrapping
black Montgomery Ward labels around the shafts,
smoothing the wrinkles. Next to me George Rayney
would be doing the same with a name brand pole—
same extruded aluminum, same wooden plug, same
plastic grip. Higher price. George would toss me
a pole and I'd toss one back and we'd grin slipping
them in the wrong boxes. Late August afternoons
the clouds would pile up, some joker would shout,
"What'd'ya think Rayney, look like rain?" Jimmy'd

turn away, say, "You wanna see rain, I'll show you rain, rot your goddam feet." He never said Vietnam. I'd tape the box shut and send it down to shipping, a temporary truce in a series of perpetual wars.

Politics Up to Date

In a nod to what the fiction writer
George Orwell called Newspeak,
the United States Congress passed
a bill forbidding states from requiring
identification of genetically modified
foods. The bill was called The Safe
and Accurate Food Labeling Act.

I go into the house and, in the dark,
write a letter to my representative
in Congress. I say political leaders
who treat people as if they are stupid
will find it difficult to govern. Not
that it's impossible, I add in a PS,
history offering the example of many
a nation made into a prison camp.
My representative doesn't answer.

A Prayer

Say a president is busy negotiating
with his third wife while also pursuing
younger women who have undergone
surgical interventions. It would be faithless
as well as foolish to have sex with them
but he does and, as myriad presidents
before and yet to come, falls from power.

We may respect a man, even a bad man,
who remains firm in the face of adversity,
but one who is too uncompromising
is hard to admire, standing in his backyard
taking pot shots at the crows roosting
in the leafless trees, listening as the silent
bodies strike the frozen earth.

Dictators brutalize love
and, in the end, they too fall.

Take heart, we're just about through.
It's been snowing all day. I'm going
outside to lift my face, open my mouth,
and let the flakes fall onto my tongue,
tasting childhood in the icy cold.

Success

You make a million
in real estate, circum-
navigate the planet
in a featherweight
aircraft, your first
novel is translated into
a thousand languages
and you find yourself
in bed with the man
of your dreams.
Or woman.
You run the New York
marathon in under
two hours. That
afternoon, having
found a cure for cancer,
you win the Nobel Prize.
And in retirement
you're elected
governor of Nevada.

It's no surprise
you feel anxious,
waiting for a fall.

Hunting

When I was fourteen, a friend's dad
took me hunting. Really, he was getting me away
from my father, a mean and unpredictable man—
tongue lashings, the belt. If my father had run
the government, we'd have all been refugees
streaming across a swollen river to a distant land,
everything we owned strapped to our backs.

We came to a cabin in the woods.
My friend's dad pressed his hand to my chest
to say, "Stop," while silently mouthing, "be quiet."
A man sat motionless on the porch.

A songbird dropped from a tree and perched
on the man's shoulder, turning its head
side to side, leaning toward the man's ear
as if to reveal a secret or tell a joke.
My hands and feet were cold.
I coughed, and the bird was gone.

Someone still sits waiting.
Someone may yet drop from the tree.

Poor People

You think I write these little poems
for pleasure? I do, and also think
they may do some good. At least,
reading them a person can't be out
making money. As for the world,
you could shoot yourself in the foot
to get out of the war. Jesus said to
love our neighbors. He might have
meant love them into submission
but it's unlikely. When people
give you advice, nod your head
and say, "Yes, I'll think about that"
then drift off into non sequiturs.
Life is personal. Even our enemies
suffer pain and loss. Doesn't mean
we should ask them to the movies.
These are the high cliffs of my soul,
the ocean waves grinding stones
to sand, the stars' light reaching us
long after the stars are dead. Often
the poorest person is most giving,
sharing half of nothing which is
quite a lot. I'm just chatting,
not telling you what to do.

There Is No

Eighty-one is the last poem
in the *Tao Te Ching*. Lao-tzu
concludes with "By not dominating,
the Master leads." And that's that.

It's over. Some readers may scratch
their heads wondering what the dickens
or may simply yawn, close what is,
after all, a short book, and go to bed.

If you want to stay up all night,
read *War and Peace* or *Moby-Dick*.
But set an alarm, just to make sure
you wake up in time to get to work.

CPSIA information can be obtained
at www.ICGtesting.com
Printed in the USA
LVHW090716100121
676130LV00004B/359